Piano and Laylee

Help a Copycat Become a Creative Cat

Carmela N. Curatola Knowles

Emily Lewellen, illustrator

S0-AQK-727

HomePage Books. HomePage Books is an imprint of the International Society for Technology in Education

EUGENE, OREGON · WASHINGTON, DC

Director of Book Publishing: Courtney Burkholder
Acquisitions Editor: Jeff V. Bolkan
Production Editors: Tina Wells, Lynda Gansel
Production Coordinator: Rachel Williams
Graphic Designer: Signe Landin

Library of Congress Cataloging-in-Publication Data

Curatola Knowles, Carmela N.
 Piano and Laylee help a copycat become a creative cat / Carmela N. Curatola Knowles ; illustrated by Emily Lewellen. — 1st ed.
    p. cm. — (A Piano and Laylee learning adventure)
 Summary: "Puppy friends Piano and Laylee teach their kitty friend Coco why it's wrong to copy others' work online and encourage her to be creative instead"—Provided by publisher.
 ISBN 978-1-56484-295-4 (hardback) — ISBN 978-1-56484-280-0 (pbk.)
 1. Copyright—Juvenile literature. 2. Fair use (Copyright)—Juvenile literature. 3. Copyright and electronic data processing—Juvenile literature. I. Lewellen, Emily, ill. II. Title.
 Z551.C87 2011
 346.04'82—dc22

                                                                                    2011011129

International Society for Technology in Education

Washington, DC, Office: 1710 Rhode Island Ave. NW, Suite 900, Washington, DC 20036-3132
Eugene, Oregon, Office: 180 West 8th Ave., Suite 300, Eugene, OR 97401-2916
Order Desk: 1.800.336.5191 • **Web:** www.iste.org

First Edition
Paperback ISBN: 978-1-56484-280-0
Hardback ISBN: 978-1-56484-295-4

Printed in the United States of America

Flower image (pgs 5–23): © iStockphoto.com/Jolanta Dabrowska

Dedicated to my brothers, Anthony and Robert, and my sisters-in-law, Patty and Diane, who are never more than a phone call away

"Copy and paste, copy and paste, I'm so great at copy and paste," sang Coco as she admired her computer work.

"There! Another excellent birthday card!" she said.

"Hi, Coco," said Laylee, as she and Piano entered Coco's family room. "What are you doing?"

"Hi, Laylee! Hi, Piano!"
Coco replied. "I'm making
a birthday card for Spike.
Isn't this a great flower?"

"It sure is," said Piano.
"In fact, it looks perfect.
Did you draw it
yourself, Coco?"

"Well, no. But this is just
a birthday card for Spike,
and this flower was exactly
what I wanted. I copied it.
Isn't it cute?" said Coco.

"Yes," Piano said. "But remember what our teacher told us at school? Copying other people's work is not okay. There's something called copyright."

"Someone took the time to paint that flower. The artist deserves to make money. Artists need to provide homes and food for their families," said Piano.

"Copying that picture is like stealing. It's not your work!" Laylee added.

Laylee continued,
"Remember, the teacher
told us that for school work
it's all right to use a small
amount of someone else's
words, pictures, music,
or movies."

HAPPY BIRTHDAY Spike!

"What's a small amount?" asked Coco.

"Ten percent or less," Laylee replied. "That's the same as one-tenth, or 10 words out of 100 words. For a song or a video, it's usually about 30 seconds."

Coco frowned and then spoke, "Why only for school work? That doesn't seem fair with so many great pictures online."

Laylee explained, "Because of something called Fair Use, Coco. It means that students can use pieces of other people's work to help them create their own ideas for school work."

Piano then added, "It also says that you have to give credit to the original author or artist."

Now Coco was interested.
"How do I do that?"
she asked.

"By typing whose work
you used and also where
you found it," said Piano.
"It would look like this."

Piano typed:

Artist: Queenie Cat

http://schools.clipart.com.
Retrieved on 10/9/2011.

CLIP ART!

"Thanks for reminding me, Piano and Laylee," said Coco. "I think I'll make my own flower on the computer for Spike."

"Great! Instead of being Coco the Copycat, you're being Coco the Creative Cat!" said Laylee.

Piano and Laylee always remember the copyright guidelines for students:

In your school work, it's okay to use a little bit of other people's music, pictures, and words.

Always give credit to the original author or artist.

Don't be a copycat!
Be a creative cat!

Carmela N. Curatola Knowles is a technology integration specialist for Hatboro-Horsham School District in Pennsylvania and a 2006 Pennsylvania Keystone Technology Integrator. She presents on technology integration at regional and international conferences and has been published in *Learning & Leading with Technology* magazine.

Emily Lewellen, the owner of Studio Squirrel Graphic Design, has a degree in applied visual arts in graphic design from Oregon State University. A mother of two, this is Lewellen's first foray into children's book illustrations.

A **Piano** and **Laylee** Learning Adventure

www.iste.org/bookstore